No More Homework! No More Tests!

Kids' Favorite Funny School Poems

Illustrated by
STEPHEN CARPENTER

Selected by
BRUCE LANSKY

SCHOLASTIC INC.

New York Toronto London Auckland Sydney

ISBN 0-590-03229-1

Published by Scholastic Inc., 555 Broadway, New York, NY 10012, by arrangement with Meadowbrook Press.

12 11 10 9 8 7 6 5 4 3 2 1   8 9/9 0 1 2 3/0

Printed in the U.S.A.   23
First Scholastic printing, January 1998

CONTENTS

INTRODUCTION

I asked more than one hundred elementary-school teachers to help me find the fifty funniest poems about school ever written. The poems in this book are the ones their students liked best.

I don't suppose that anyone will be surprised to find their favorite poems by Shel Silverstein, Jack Prelutsky, Kalli Dakos, David L. Harrison, Max Fatchen, Colin McNaughton, Carol Diggory Shields, or Bobbi Katz in this anthology. Nor will readers who are familiar with my earlier anthologies, *Kids Pick the Funniest Poems* and *A Bad Case of the Giggles*, be surprised to find their favorite poems by Bill Dodds, Joyce Armor, Robert Scotellaro, Helen Ksypka, Timothy Tocher, and Rebecca Kai Dotlich.

But I'm embarrassed that so many of the poems in this book are mine. When you test poems on kids, you never know what will happen. If we had tested poems on goats, I suppose the results would have been completely different. They would have eaten the poems.

I hope that you grin, giggle, and guffaw while reading these poems as much as the kids who tested them.

Happy reading,

Bruce Lansky

ACKNOWLEDGMENTS

I want to thank the more than one hundred teachers and more than three thousand students who helped me select the poems for this book over a period of seven years. Although I cannot possibly mention everyone, here is a brief list of teachers who helped us make the final selections:

Shirley Hallquist, Pinewood Elementary School; Jeanne M. Nelsen, St. Mary's Catholic School; Barb Rannigan, Alta Vista Elementary School; Ron Sangalang, Sherwood Forest Elementary School; Mary Jane Savino, Barton School; Suzanne Thompson, Holy Name of Jesus Catholic School; and Lynette Townsend, Lomarena Elementary School.

Look Out!

The witches mumble horrid chants,
You're scolded by five thousand aunts,
   A Martian pulls a fearsome face
   And hurls you into Outer Space,
You're tied in front of whistling trains,
A tomahawk has sliced your brains,
   The tigers snarl, the giants roar,
   You're sat on by a dinosaur.
In vain you're shouting "Help" and "Stop,"
The walls are spinning like a top,
   The earth is melting in the sun
   And all the horror's just begun.
And, oh, the screams, the thumping hearts—
That awful night before school starts.

Max Fatchen

... Keep your elbows
off the table...

Monday!

Overslept
Rain is pouring
Missed the bus
Dad is roaring
Late for school
Forgot my spelling
Soaking wet
Clothes are smelling
Dropped my books
Got them muddy

Flunked a test
Didn't study
Teacher says
I must do better
Lost my money
Tore my sweater
Feeling dumber
Feeling glummer
Monday sure can be
A bummer.

David L. Harrison

School Daze Rap

Woke up at eight—oh no, I overslept!
I ran for the bus, but the bus had left.
I raced to school, I really, really buzzed,
But then I forgot where my classroom was.
Finally found it, opened the door—
My teacher turned into a dinosaur!
The dinosaur roared, "Sit down at your desk!
Pick up your pencil, 'cause we're having a test!"
All the kids were staring, sitting in their rows,
I looked down and saw I'd forgotten my clothes.
The dinosaur frowned and started to shake me,
Turned into my mom, who was trying to wake me.
"Hey, sleepyhead, Tommy's here to play,
Why aren't you up? It's Saturday."

Carol Diggory Shields

Don't Pinch!

When I got on the school bus,
I was in for a surprise.
My friends all stared and pointed.
There was mischief in their eyes.

A kid who sat in front of me
reached out and pinched my knee.
My friends all started laughing,
but the joke was lost on me.

And then I got a second pinch.
I felt it on my ear.
And then I felt a third and fourth.
You guessed it—on my rear.

I asked, "Why are you pinching me?
I think it's very mean!"
They said, "Today's St. Patrick's Day
and you're not wearing green."

Bruce Lansky

Morning Announcements

Good morning, staff and students.
Take note of what I say.
In school we will have showers,
for April starts today.

Some teachers were suspended
for giving too much work.
Today, if you feel lazy,
you'll be allowed to shirk.

We want to find the student
who brought a pig to school.
It is *running* down the hallways,
and that's against the rule.

Today on our lunch menu
are bumblebees in sauce
or chopped-cockroach sandwiches
and salad you can toss.

Next year we'll pay our students
for work they do in school . . .
and if you believe these messages,
then you're an APRIL FOOL!

Sylvia Andrews

English Is a Pain! (Pane?)

Rain, reign, rein,
English is a pain.
Although the words
sound just alike,
the spelling's not the same!

Bee, be, B,
I'd rather climb a tree
than learn to spell
the same old word,
not just one way, but three!

Sight, site, cite,
I try with all my might.
No matter which
I finally choose,
it's not the one that's right!

There, their, they're,
enough to make you swear.
Too many ways
to write one sound,
I just don't think it's fair!

To, two, too,
so what's a kid to do?
I think I'll go
to live on Mars
and leave this mess with ewe!
(you?)

Shirlee Curlee Bingham

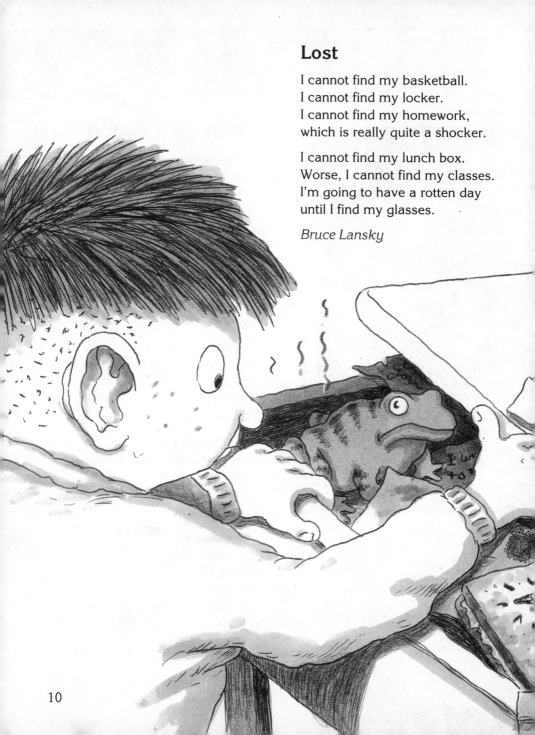

Lost

I cannot find my basketball.
I cannot find my locker.
I cannot find my homework,
which is really quite a shocker.

I cannot find my lunch box.
Worse, I cannot find my classes.
I'm going to have a rotten day
until I find my glasses.

Bruce Lansky

10

What I Found in My Desk

A ripe peach with an ugly bruise,
a pair of stinky tennis shoes,
a day-old ham-and-cheese on rye,
a swimsuit that I left to dry,
a pencil that glows in the dark,
some bubble gum found in the park,
a paper bag with cookie crumbs,
an old kazoo that barely hums,
a spelling test I almost failed,
a letter that I should have mailed,
and one more thing, I must confess,
a note from teacher: Clean This Mess!!!!

Bruce Lansky

A Bad Case of the Giggles

I found a book of poems.
I brought the book to school.
And every time I read it,
I giggle like a fool.

Today in social studies,
I opened up the book.
I started giggling right away
from just a single look.

I'm croaking like a bullfrog.
I'm braying like a mule.
These aren't sounds you're supposed to make
while studying at school.

The more I try to stop it,
the louder that I howl.
I'm squawking like a parrot,
and hooting like an owl!

I'm making a commotion;
the teacher is upset.
I'm losing my position
as teacher's favorite pet!

My giggling is contagious.
My friends have all joined in.
The teacher's getting angry.
We're making quite a din.

The whole darned class is giggling.
Not one of us can stop.
The teacher says that if we can't,
he'll call the hallway cop.

The room next door has heard us.
And now they're giggling too.
The sound of giggling travels fast.
The school sounds like a zoo.

And now the teacher's giving up.
He cannot teach today.
The principal's declaring it
a giggling holiday.

Bruce Lansky

Clear As Mud

I go to bed each morning.
I wake up every night.
I spill my milk at breakfast,
and then turn on the light.

Each day I miss the school bus.
I never have been late.
I don't turn in my homework.
My teacher thinks I'm great.

My favorite game is basketball.
I cannot sink a shot.
We haven't won a single game.
Our team is getting hot!

Last year I was in high school.
Now I'm in second grade.
Next year I'll be in daycare.
I'll really have it made!

When I grow up, I'm hoping
a baby I can be:
a pacifier in my mouth,
my cradle in a tree.

This poem's so confusing.
It's all so crystal clear.
Perhaps I'll understand it,
when I am born next year.

Bruce Lansky

What's So Funny?

There's something no one's telling me.
There's something I don't know.
I notice people staring at me
everywhere I go.

I ask my friends to clue me in;
not knowing is distressing.
But no one says a single word;
I find that quite depressing.

They point at me and giggle.
They point at me and grin.
I'll have to find out just what kind
of trouble I am in.

I check the bathroom mirror
to learn the awful truth.
I find a piece of lettuce
sticking on my big front tooth.

I rinse the yucky green away.
I think that is the end.
But then I hear more giggling—
it comes from my best friend.

I tell him, "Jack, please help me out,
I'm feeling kind of blue."
He says, "You've got some toilet paper
sticking to your shoe!"

Bruce Lansky

Brain Drain

The dinosaurs did not remain
Because they had a tiny brain.
But recently, our teacher found
That tiny brains are still around . . .

Max Fatchen

Recess

Suzy banged her elbow,
Samantha skinned her knee,
Jamie tore her sweatshirt,
Inez fell from a tree,
Harry got a bee sting,
and Aaron ran away.
Now you know why schools have
just one recess a day.

Timothy Tocher

Could Have Been Worse

My friends have not seen London,
They've never been to France,
But yesterday at recess
They saw my underpants.

I kicked a ball, my skirt flew up,
And I know what they saw.
The girls all stared and blushed and laughed,
The boys said, "Oo-la-la!"

I've thought a lot about it.
This conclusion I have drawn:
I'm embarrassed that they saw them,
But I'm glad I had them on.

Bill Dodds

Mary Had Some Bubble Gum

Mary had some bubble gum,
she chewed it long and slow,
and everywhere that Mary went
her gum was sure to go.
She chewed the gum in school one day,
which was against the rule.
The teacher took her pack away
and chewed it after school.

Anonymous

Teacher's Pet

Call a doctor.
Call the vet!
I've just been bitten
By teacher's pet!

Colin McNaughton

Norman Norton's Nostrils

Oh, Norman Norton's nostrils
Are powerful and strong;
Hold on to your belongings
If he should come along.

And do not ever let him
Inhale with all his might,
Or else your pens and pencils
Will disappear from sight.

Right up his nose they'll vanish.
Your future will be black.
Unless he gets the sneezes
You'll *never* get them back.

Colin West

Gloria

Gloria was perfect
In lots of little ways.
She had at least a million friends
And always got straight A's.
I think she was the cutest girl
That I have ever met:
The apple of her mother's eye
And every teacher's pet.

But then one day it happened.
The unthinkable, to wit:
Gloria the Perfect
Got a king-sized zit!
Big and red and puffy,
It covered half her brow.
Funny thing about it, though—
I like her better now.

Joyce Armor

Eddie Edwards

Eddie Edwards runs around.
He never shuts up, he never sits down.
He teases the girls, he cuts in line,
He never makes it to school on time.

Eddie Edwards does sound effects,
Like sirens and lasers and racing-car wrecks.
His pen has a leak, his binder's a mess,
And you wouldn't believe what he keeps in his desk.

Eddie Edwards' socks don't match.
His hair looks like a blackberry patch.
His shoelaces dangle like dirty spaghetti,
And I wish that I could be just like Eddie.

Carol Diggory Shields

Amanda

I think Amanda likes me.
I think Amanda cares.
Today she kicked my lunch box
Halfway down the stairs.

I think Amanda likes me.
I think it's really true.
At the hallway fountain
She spit water on my shoe.

I think Amanda likes me.
I knew it when she said
She thinks I'm gross, disgusting,
And a total cootie-head.

Carol Diggory Shields

Most Outstanding Students of the Year Awards*

I'm making this announcement
to honor _____ best.
         [school's name]
I think that you will all agree
they rose above the rest.

Our most outstanding artist
is Christopher McKnight.
He's the one who painted all the
classroom blackboards white.

Our most outstanding sportsman
is Stephen Montague.
He scored a basket for his team—
and the opponents', too.

*Fill in the blanks with the
  name of your school.*

28

The student teachers like the best
is Alexander Brash.
Most kids give teachers apples.
But Alex gave them cash.

The winner for attendance
is Mary Anne McKay.
She came to school on every day
of Christmas holiday.

Congratulations, winners!
Let's all give them a cheer—
the _____ Elementary
      [school's name]
students of the year.

Bruce Lansky

New Year's Resolutions

Last year I did some rotten things.
This year I will be better.
Here are some resolutions
I will follow to the letter:

I won't make dumb excuses
when my homework isn't done;
when the truth is that I did no work
'cause I was having fun.

I won't fly paper airplanes
when the teacher isn't looking.
I won't sneak in the kitchen
just to taste what they are cooking.

I will not twist the silverware
to see how far it bends.
I will not take the candy bars
from lunch bags of my friends.

I will not skateboard down the hall
or skateboard down the stairs.
I won't run over teachers,
and I won't crash into chairs.

I will not do these rotten things;
my heart is full of sorrow.
But I have got some brand-new tricks
to try in school tomorrow.

Bruce Lansky

31

My Sister's Always on the Phone

My sister's always on the phone.
I never see her study.
She doesn't do her homework,
which is why her grades are cruddy.

My sister's always on the phone,
but I don't think that's cool.
My sister is so popular
she's flunking out of school.

Bruce Lansky

A Teacher's Lament

Don't tell me the cat ate your math sheet,
And your spelling words went down the drain,
And you couldn't decipher your homework,
Because it was soaked in the rain.

Don't tell me you slaved for hours
On the project that's due today,
And you would have had it finished
If your snake hadn't run away.

Don't tell me you lost your eraser,
And your worksheets and pencils, too,
And your papers are stuck together
With a great big glob of glue.

I'm tired of all your excuses;
They are really a terrible bore.
Besides, I forgot my own work,
At home in my study drawer.

Kalli Dakos

Confession

I have a brief confession
that I would like to make.
If I don't get it off my chest
I'm sure my heart will break.

I didn't do my reading.
I watched TV instead—
while munching cookies, cakes, and chips
and cinnamon raisin bread.

I didn't wash the dishes.
I didn't clean the mess.
Now there are roaches eating crumbs—
a million, more or less.

I didn't turn the TV off.
I didn't shut the light.
Just think of all the energy
I wasted through the night.

I feel so very guilty.
I did a lousy job.
I hope my students don't find out
that I am such a slob.

Bruce Lansky

The Creature in the Classroom

It appeared inside our classroom
at a quarter after ten,
it gobbled up the blackboard,
three erasers and a pen.
It gobbled teacher's apple
and it bopped her with the core.
"How dare you!" she responded.
"You must leave us . . . there's the door."

The Creature didn't listen
but described an arabesque
as it gobbled all her pencils,
seven notebooks and her desk.
Teacher stated very calmly,
"Sir! You simply cannot stay,
I'll report you to the principal
unless you go away!"

But the thing continued eating,
it ate paper, swallowed ink,
as it gobbled up our homework
I believe I saw it wink.
Teacher finally lost her temper.
"OUT!" she shouted at the creature.
The creature hopped beside her
and GLOPP . . . it gobbled teacher.

Jack Prelutsky

How to Torture Your Teacher

Only raise your hand when
you want to sharpen your pencil
or go to the bathroom.
Repeat every ten minutes.

Never raise your hand
when you want to answer a question;
instead, yell, "Oooh! Oooh! Oooh!"
and then, when the teacher calls on you,
say, "I forgot what I was going to say."

Lean your chair back,
take off your shoes, and
put your feet up on your desk.
Act surprised when the teacher
puts all four legs of your chair back on the floor.

Drop the eraser end of your pencil
on your desk.
See how high it will bounce.

Drop your books on the floor.
See how loud a noise you can make.

Hum.
Get all your friends to join in.

Hold your nose,
make a face, and say, "P.U.!"
Fan the air away from your face,
and point to the kid in front of you.

On the last day of school,
lead your classmates in chanting:
"No more pencils!
No more books!
No more teachers'
dirty looks!"

Then, on your way out
the door, tell the teacher,
"Bet you're looking forward
to summer vacation this year.
But I'll sure miss you.
You're the best teacher
I've ever had."

Bruce Lansky

There's a New Cook in the Cafeteria

Good morning, staff and students.
We have a brand new cook.
And that's why our lunch menu
will have a brand new look.

To make a good impression,
our cook's prepared a treat:
your choice of snapping turtle soup
or deep-fried monkey meat.

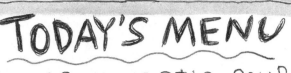

TODAY'S MENU
- SNAPPING TURTLE SOUP
- DEEP FRIED MONKEY MEAT
- PICKLED CAULIFLOWER
- JELLYFISH SOUFFLE
- CHOCOLATE COVERED ANTS

If you're a vegetarian,
we have good news today:
she's serving pickled cauliflower
and jellyfish soufflé.

And for dessert our cook has made
a recipe from France:
I'm sure you'll all want seconds—
of chocolate-covered ants.

I hope you like this gourmet feast.
I hope you won't complain.
But if you do we'll have to bring
our old cook back again.

Bruce Lansky

Mystery Meal

Great green globs of
greasy, grimy gopher guts,
mutilated monkey meat,
little birdies' dirty feet—
Hot school lunches
aren't fit for kids to eat,
so pass the ketchup please.

Bruce Lansky

What's This?

It's gunky goo, a slimy stew
of runny, drippy glop
or mucky mounds of icky, sticky,
greasy, grimy slop.

It's heaps of slush—a mass of mush
or gobs of gluey lumps,
unappetizing drops and plops
of culinary clumps.

It sometimes, too, is hard to chew
when brittle as a brick,
cuisine that has a dose of gross—
enough to make you sick.

With every clue I've given you,
I'm sure you have a hunch.
It's what they have the nerve to serve
at school and call it "lunch."

Helen Ksypka

The Monster Who Ate at Our School Cafeteria

A monster used to eating
slime gumbo from a ditch,
and worm goo, lightly salted,
and slugs sautéed in pitch

came into our school lunchroom
and filled his tray up quick,
with food they serve us daily—
it made the monster sick!

He held his aching belly,
then hollored out, quite gruff,
"I'd rather give up eating
than eat this gruesome stuff!"

Robert Scotellaro

Bring Your Own Lunch

Don't eat school lunches—
not even a lick.
They might make you nauseous.
They might make you sick.

Just take a small bite and
you'll start to feel ill.
If the veggies don't get you,
the meatloaf sure will.

Bruce Lansky

45

No More Flies in the School Kitchen

There were lots of flies in the kitchen.
The cook didn't know what to do.
The principal made an inspection.
He swatted some flies with his shoe.

Now there are no flies in the kitchen.
The cook's in a very good mood.
The flies are not quite so delighted.
They died after eating the food.

Bruce Lansky

How to Eat a Bag Lunch

Banana:
Remove Chiquita
sticker, slap your
friend's back, say, "Ho,
ho, ho," and leave
sticker stuck to shirt.

Cupcake:
Lick off frosting, being
careful to smear it
around mouth and on
chin. Do not eat the
cupcake; crumble it.

Potato Chips:
Leaving out two kids
who are sitting at the
table, give one chip to
kids you like. Prefer to
eat chips with hardly
any brown in them.

Straw:
Shoot off paper, aiming
at the cafeteria
monitor.

Drumstick:
Brag about having fried
chicken. Say that you
had it last night for
dinner. Say that you
have fried chicken at
your house three times
a week, easy.

Announce your favorite part. Wave the drumstick while chanting, "Roast chicken, boo; fried chicken, yay." Pick off skin with fingers; then consume.

Milk:
After spilling, throw carton in garbage can as if it were a basketball. Then move sideways on the bench, shoving the person next to you until the kid at the other end falls off.

Hard-Boiled Egg:
Do not eat, but leave the peeled-off shell and bare egg covered with dirty fingerprints on the cafeteria table.

Paper Bag:
Blow in air, hold closed, and smash. Spend the rest of lunch sitting with the little kids.

Delia Ephron

Excuses, Excuses

I couldn't do my homework.
I had asthma and was wheezing.
I had nosebleeds, measles, heat rash,
with some very painful sneezing,
and itchy skin with blisters—
oh so blotchy red and hivy—
malaria and toothaches,
and a patch of poison ivy,
eight spider bites and hair loss,
and a broken leg with scabies,
Rocky Mountain spotted fever,
and a full-blown case of rabies.
I suffered—it was awful—
but I'm feeling better now.
Could I have done my homework?
No, I really don't see how.

Joyce Armor

Too Busy

I've folded all my laundry
and put it in the drawer.
I've changed my linen, made my bed,
and swept my bedroom floor.

I've emptied out the garbage
and fixed tomorrow's lunch.
I've baked some cookies for dessert
and given dad a munch.

I've searched the house for pencils
and sharpened every one.
There are so many things to do
when homework must be done.

Bruce Lansky

A Remarkable Adventure

I was at my bedroom table
with a notebook open wide,
when a giant anaconda
started winding up my side,
I was filled with apprehension
and retreated down the stairs,
to be greeted at the bottom
by a dozen grizzly bears.

We tumultuously tussled
till I managed to get free,
then I saw, with trepidation,
there were tigers after me,
I could feel them growing closer,
I was quivering with fear,
then I blundered into quicksand
and began to disappear.

I was rescued by an eagle
that descended from the skies
to embrace me with its talons,
to my terror and surprise,
but that raptor lost its purchase
when a blizzard made me sneeze,
and it dropped me in a thicket
where I battered both my knees.

I was suddenly surrounded
by a troop of savage trolls,
who maliciously informed me
they would toast me over coals,
I was lucky to elude them
when they briefly looked away—
that's the reason why my homework
isn't here with me today.

Jack Prelutsky

Why My Homework Is Late

Broke my nose.
Stubbed my toe.
Dropped my notebook in the snow.
Roof blew off.
Walls caved in.
Rusty scissors stabbed my chin.
Bit my tongue.
Choked on bones.
Caught a cold and kidney stones.
Had a boil.
Had a blister.
Had to babysit my sister.
Had the measles.
Had the pox.
Tonsils swelled up big as rocks.
Lost my watch.
Forgot the date.
And *that* is why my homework's late!

Rebecca Kai Dotlich

My Dog Chewed Up My Homework

I'm glad to say my homework's done.
I finished it last night.
I've got it right here in this box.
It's not a pretty sight.

My dog chewed up my homework.
He slobbered on it, too.
So now my homework's ripped to shreds
and full of slimy goo.

It isn't much to look at,
but I brought it anyway.
I'm going to dump it on your desk
if I don't get an A.

Bruce Lansky

Freddie

I don't like doing homework.
I know that it will bore me.
But now I am much happier
'Cause Freddie does it for me!

He greets me at the door each day
When I come home from school.
He just can't wait to read my books—
I think that's pretty cool.

I give him all my homework,
Like history and math.
And when he's done I give him
A nice warm bubble bath!

My grades are so much better now,
Which makes my parents glad.
Freddie is the smartest dog
That I have ever had!

Phil Bolsta

56

I Love to Do My Homework

I love to do my homework.
It makes me feel so good.
I love to do exactly
as my teacher says I should.

I love to do my homework.
I never miss a day.
I even love the men in white
who are taking me away.

Anonymous

Homework! Oh, Homework!

Homework! Oh, homework!
I hate you! You stink!
I wish I could wash you
away in the sink,
if only a bomb
would explode you to bits.
Homework! Oh, homework!
You're giving me fits.

I'd rather take baths
with a man-eating shark,
or wrestle a lion
alone in the dark,
eat spinach and liver,
pet ten porcupines,
than tackle the homework
my teacher assigns.

Homework! Oh, homework!
You're last on my list,
I simply can't see
why you even exist,
if you just disappeared
it would tickle me pink.
Homework! Oh, homework!
I hate you! You stink!

Jack Prelutsky

Measles

There are measles on my forehead.
There are measles on my nose.
There are measles on my elbows.
There are measles on my toes.

There are measles on the carpet.
There are measles on the chair.
There are measles on my glasses.
There are measles in my hair.

I'm so tired of painting measles.
I would like to take a rest.
I sure hope I have enough to be
excused from tomorrow's test.

Bruce Lansky

61

Difficult Math Test

Whoopie! A test! Whoopie! A test!
We're having a difficult test!
We'd also enjoy being kicked by a mule,
then dipped in a caldron of bubbling drool,
but a difficult test is best!

A woodpecker pecking a tune on your head,
then trapped in a mighty collapsible bed,
or dancing barefooted with ol' Frankenstein,
sure, all of these things, why of course, would be fine,
but a difficult test is best!

Or baked in a pie in an oven too hot,
and having your fingers all tied in a knot,
then using a chair made of porcupine quills,
can also provide you a great deal of thrills,
but a difficult test is best!

Or put in a vise and then squeezed till you're flat,
or sharing your room with a twenty-foot rat,
and then wearing some tight cactus underwear,
but none of, no none of these things can compare
to the joys of a difficult test!

Robert Scotellaro

A Student's Prayer

Now I lay me down to rest.
I pray I pass tomorrow's test.
If I should die before I wake,
that's one less test I'll have to take.

Anonymous

I Should Have Studied

I didn't study for the test
and now I'm feeling blue.
I copied off your paper
and I flunked it just like you.

Bruce Lansky

Sick

"I cannot go to school today,"
Said little Peggy Ann McKay.
"I have the measles and the mumps,
A gash, a rash and purple bumps.
My mouth is wet, my throat is dry,
I'm going blind in my right eye.
My tonsils are as big as rocks,
I've counted sixteen chicken pox
And there's one more—that's seventeen,
And don't you think my face looks green?
My leg is cut, my eyes are blue—
It might be instamatic flu.
I cough and sneeze and gasp and choke,
I'm sure that my left leg is broke—
My hip hurts when I move my chin,
My belly button's caving in,
My back is wrenched, my ankle's sprained,
My 'pendix pains each time it rains.
My nose is cold, my toes are numb,
I have a sliver in my thumb.
My neck is stiff, my voice is weak,
I hardly whisper when I speak.
My tongue is filling up my mouth,
I think my hair is falling out.
My elbow's bent, my spine ain't straight,
My temperature is one-o-eight.
My brain is shrunk, I cannot hear,
There is a hole inside my ear.
I have a hangnail, and my heart is—what?
What's that? What's that you say?
You say today is . . . Saturday?
G'bye, I'm going out to play!"

Shel Silverstein

66

Today Is Not a Good Day

Today is not a good day.
I woke up sick in bed.
My stomach has a stabbing pain
that's spreading to my head.
My knees are weak and achy.
My eyes are full of flu.
I fear I may contaminate;
I have a fever too.
I cannot see.
I cannot breathe.
I cannot read or write.
My eyes are shut.
My nose is blocked.
I'm not a pretty sight.
I cannot lift a finger
or move a tired toe.
My throat is hot and scratchy.
The answer's simply NO . . .
I cannot go to school today;
I'm awfully sorry too,
this had to happen on the day
my book report was due.

Rebecca Kai Dotlich

The Teachers' Show*

I have an important announcement.
I want everybody to know:
on Monday all classes are cancelled.
The teachers will put on a show.

_____ will be juggling meatballs.
[Teacher's name]

_____ will dance with a bear.
[Teacher's name]

_____ and _____ will yodel.
[Teacher's name]   [Teacher's name]

_____ will tear out _____ hair.
[Teacher's name]   [his or her]

_____ is quite entertaining.
[Teacher's name]

_____ does something you've never seen.
[He or She]

If you want a bad case of measles,

_____ paint them on red, white, and green.
[He'll or She'll]

_____ is also performing.
[Principal's name]

_____ come up with something quite new.
[He's or She's]

_____ doing _____ act in the kitchen.
[He's or She's]   [his or her]

_____ dumping the cook in the stew.
[He's or She's]

Your parents are certainly welcome,
but make sure to tell them the rule:
If any of them arrive tardy,
they'll have to be kept after school.

I know that our show is exciting.
I wish that you all could be here.
But school will be closed for vacation.
I can't wait to see you next year.

Bruce Lansky

**Fill in the blanks with
the names of teachers
in your school.*

School, Some Suggestions

If kids could be the teachers,
if kids could make the rules,
there'd be a lot of changes made
in almost all the schools.
First thing they'd stop the homework.
They'd never give a test.
They know that growing children
must have their proper rest.
They'd make the lunchtime longer—
let's say from twelve to two,
so every growing boy or girl
had time enough to chew!

Of course, concerning recess,
kids clearly realize
to keep their bodies healthy,
kids need to exercise.
And so there would be recess,
perhaps from nine to ten,
and then when it is two o'clock
it's recess time again!
With longer, stronger weekends,
each child would grow so smart—
he would perform with excellence
in music, gym, and art!

Bobbi Katz

Class Dismissed

(sing to the tune of "The Battle Hymn of the Republic")

We have broken all the blackboards
so the teachers cannot write.
We have painted all the toilets black
and all the lockers white.

We have torn up all the math books
and we've locked the school's front door.
There won't be school no more.

Glory, glory hallelujah!
School is closed now, what's it to ya?
There won't be no more homework
and there won't be no more tests.
There won't be school no more.

Bruce Lansky

CREDITS

AUTHOR INDEX